91130000023673

D0653775

EXTREME

Mummies

Mysteries of the Ancient World

Paul Harrison

A&C Black • London

BRENT LIBRARIES
91130000023673
PETERS 16-Feb-2010
£11.50 BRTOW
CNF

Produced for A & C Black by
Monkey Puzzle Media Ltd
Little Manor Farm, Brundish,
Woodbridge, Suffolk IP13 8BL, UK

Published by A & C Black Publishers Limited
36 Soho Square, London W1D 3QY

First published 2009
Copyright © 2009 A & C Black Publishers Limited

ISBN 978-1-4081-1260-1 (hardback)
ISBN 978-1-4081-1998-4 (paperback)

All rights reserved. No part of this publication may be reproduced, stored in a retrieval system or transmitted in any form, electronic, mechanical, photocopying, recording or otherwise, without prior permission of A & C Black Publishers Limited.

The right of Paul Harrison to be identified as the author of this Work has been asserted by him in accordance with the Copyright, Designs and Patents Act 1988.

A CIP catalogue record for this book is available from the British Library.

Editor: Susie Brooks
Design: Mayer Media Ltd
Picture research: Lynda Lines
Series consultants: Jane Turner and James de Winter

This book is produced using paper that is made from wood grown in managed, sustainable forests. It is natural, renewable and recyclable. The logging and manufacturing processes conform to the environmental regulations of the country of origin.

Printed in Singapore by Tien Wah Press (Pte.) Ltd

Picture acknowledgements
Alamy pp. 18 (North Wind Picture Archives), 26–27 (Dennis Cox); Art Archive p. 26 left (Musée du Louvre, Paris/Gianni Dagli Orti); Camera Press pp. 15 (Gamma/Duclos Alexis), 17 (New China News Agency); Corbis pp. 6 bottom left (Claudio Castellon/epa), 11 (Vienna Report Agency), 14 (Chris Rainier), 28 (Ryan Pyle/None); Adam Husted p. 21; iStockphoto p. 4; MPM Images pp. 5 bottom right (Universal Pictures), 12, 16 (Smithsonian National Museum of Natural History), 24 left (University College London); National Geographic Society pp. 8 left, 8 right; Rex Features pp. 1 (Sipa Press), 10 (Sipa Press), 19 (Sipa Press), 24–25 (Sipa Press), 29 (Wotjek Laski); Science Photo Library pp. 9 (Christian Jegou/Publiphoto Diffusion), 13 (Silkeborg Museum, Denmark/Munoz-Yague), 20 (Alexander Tsiaras), 23 (British Museum/Munoz-Yague); Topfoto.co.uk p. 22; Werner Forman Archive p. 5 left (E Strouhal/Naprstek Muaseum, Prague); Wikimedia Commons pp. 6–7 (British Museum).

The front cover shows a mummy in the catacombs of Palermo, Italy (MPM Images).

Every effort has been made to contact copyright holders of material reproduced in this book. Any omissions will be rectified in subsequent printings if notice is given to the publishers.

CONTENTS

What is a mummy? 4
Air dryer 6
Making a mummy 8
Ice men 10
Bog bodies 12
Smokin' mummies 14
Good as new? 16
Mummy misery 18
Under wraps 20
Back from the dead 22
Celebrity mummies 24
Fakes and mistakes 26
Modern mummies 28
Glossary 30
Further information 31
Index 32

What is a mummy?

Mummies stumble around, wrapped in bandages, preying on human flesh – at least they do in the movies. Real life is different, but it can be just as gruesome.

Your body is designed to rot, or decompose. When you die, the **bacteria** that have been living quietly inside your body really go to town. They start to eat you – from the inside out!

The rotting process has to be stopped for a body to become a mummy. If a body is mummified it can last for thousands of years.

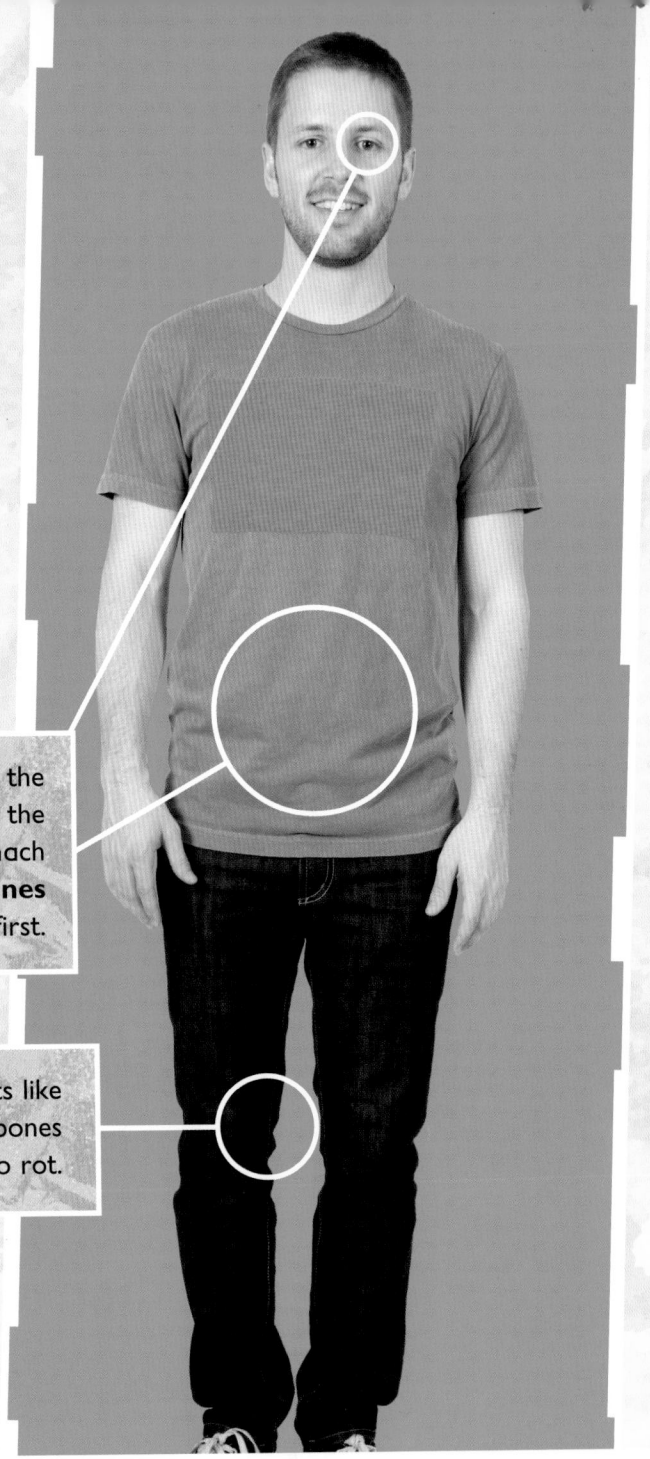

A healthy body is full of bacteria – they won't start to eat you until you're dead.

bacteria tiny cells that can both help and harm living things

Movie mummies!

In 1932, the horror movie *The Mummy* came out. Boris Karloff played an ancient Egyptian priest who had been brought back to life. Even Boris's *own* mummy wouldn't have recognized him – he was wrapped in bandages! Mummies have been a hit at the movies ever since.

She may not look that healthy, but this mummy is over 1,000 years old.

A poster for the first major mummy movie.

intestines the tube from your stomach to your bottom

Air dryer

Mummies are sometimes made by accident. If the air is dry enough, bodies dry out instead of rotting – and become mummies.

Watery wonder

Between 55 and 65 per cent of an adult human's body is made of water.

This air-dried mummy from China is curled up, just as he died.

withered dried out **preserve** to keep, or make last

If you want your body to last, then dying in a hot, dry country is a good idea. The ancient Egyptians discovered mummification when they found that bodies buried in the desert **withered** rather than rotted.

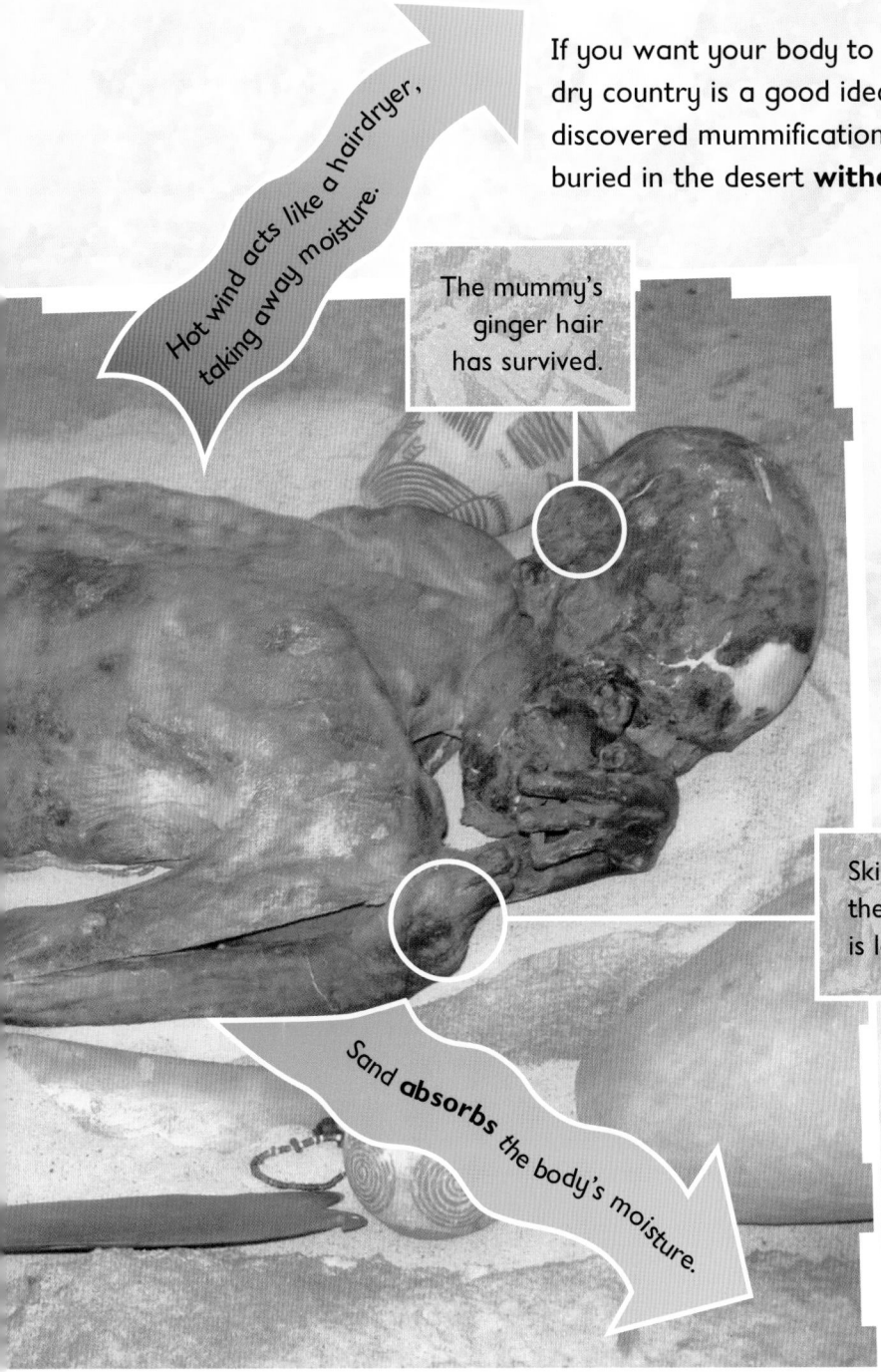

The desert mummies gave the Egyptians the basic information about how to **preserve** a body. They realized that if you get rid of a body's **moisture**, it doesn't rot. The Egyptians soon became mummy-making experts.

This mummy is known as Ginger, thanks to the colour of his hair.

moisture wetness **absorb** to soak up

Making a mummy

What do salt and a long metal hook have in common? Well, they are two of the things that the ancient Egyptians used to make bodies last for thousands of years.

Large hook pulls the brain out through the nose.

Mummification stage 1: **Organs** *such as the brain, lungs and liver contain lots of water so are removed.*

Stage 2: The body is dried out for 40 days in a salt called natron.

Poor show

Mummification was very expensive, so poor Egyptians had to make do with being buried in the sand.

organs parts of the body that do special jobs

Stage 3: The body is wrapped in bandages and prepared for burial.

The Egyptians believed that when people died, they went on to an **afterlife**. This made it important for bodies to be preserved. Mummification became a religious ceremony, carried out by priests saying prayers and casting spells.

If the whole point was to make bodies last, then the Egyptians did a great job. They had really worked out the best way of drying a body so that it wouldn't rot.

afterlife life after death

Ice men

The weather high up in the mountains is icy cold. It can have the same effect as a giant freezer when it comes to dead bodies – keeping them fresh for ages.

When two hikers found the **corpse** of a man in the Alps, they thought it was a recent body. It turned out to be a 5,300-year-old mummy! How and why he died remained a mystery for years. Eventually scientists discovered the end of a **flint** arrow buried in his shoulder, proving that the ice man had been murdered a long time ago.

In the past, people from Peru used the cold mountain air to mummify their dead relatives.

corpse a dead body **flint** a type of stone used for old tools and weapons

pollen a powdery substance that plants use to reproduce

Bog bodies

Getting trapped in a bog would be bad news – you could get sucked down and drown. On the plus side, your body might become a famous mummy!

*This bog body has been flattened by the heavy **peat**.*

Grisly secrets

Some bodies found in bogs seem to show that they had been killed as a punishment, or even sacrificed.

You'd think that a body in a really wet place like a bog would rot quickly – but that's not what happens at all. Instead bodies in bogs get pickled, like pickled onions, before they rot.

There's very little air in bog water, and the bacteria that rot bodies need air to survive. Also, the water is full of plants that make the water slightly **acid** – like the vinegar that onions are pickled in.

peat mixture of rotting plants and water **sacrificed** killed as part of a religious ceremony

"Tollund Man" lived 6,000 years ago – until he was hanged and buried in a bog.

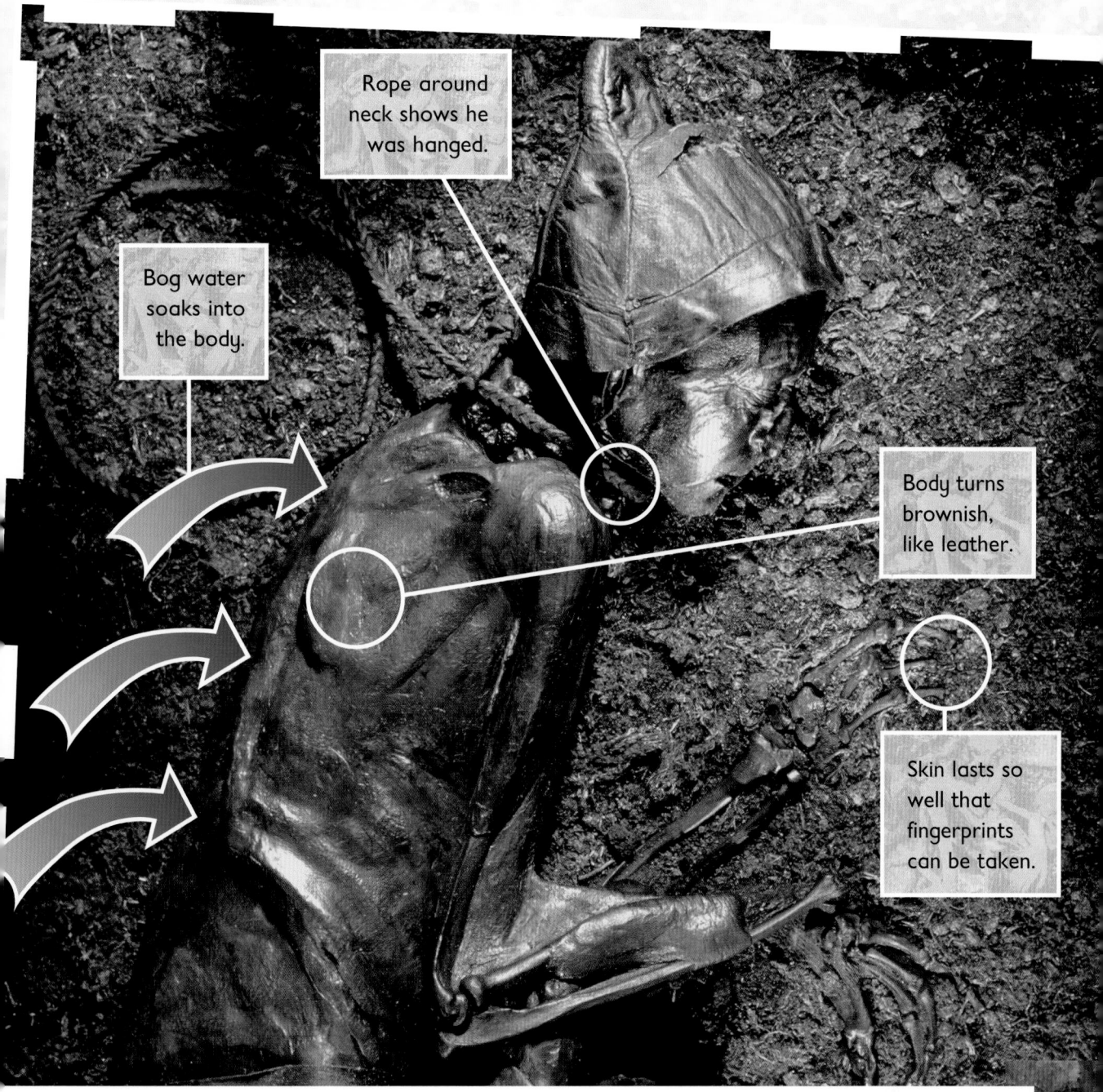

acid substance that can cause chemical changes

Smokin' mummies

Smoked mummies from Papua New Guinea do a lot of sitting around.

Death doesn't always mean saying goodbye forever. Some people mummify relatives so they can still visit them – even though they're no longer alive!

In Papua New Guinea, dead bodies are preserved using smoke – a bit like a butcher smokes ham. The mummies are then displayed in a high place that overlooks the village, or placed in local huts. In this way, the villagers feel that the dead are still part of their **community**.

Bad – and good

Tobacco smoke is bad for your health – but great for preserving dead bodies!

community a group of people who live near each other **dehydrate** to dry out

You might find a mummy like this in the mountains of the Philippines.
Tobacco smoke was blown into the corpse to dry the insides.
Tattooed skin survives.
Person drank a salty drink before death to help **dehydrate** the body.
Body was dried over a fire.

Good as new?

Imagine opening an old coffin and finding a well-preserved body inside! It sounds like a scene from a vampire movie, but it can really happen.

Fangtastic tales

Vampire legends might have their roots in the discovery of well-preserved adipocere corpses.

A coffin and where it is buried can have surprising effects on a corpse – especially if an **airtight** coffin is buried in damp, cold ground. In these conditions, the fats inside the body can turn into a waxy or soap-like substance called adipocere. This can make the body look as if it has stopped rotting altogether.

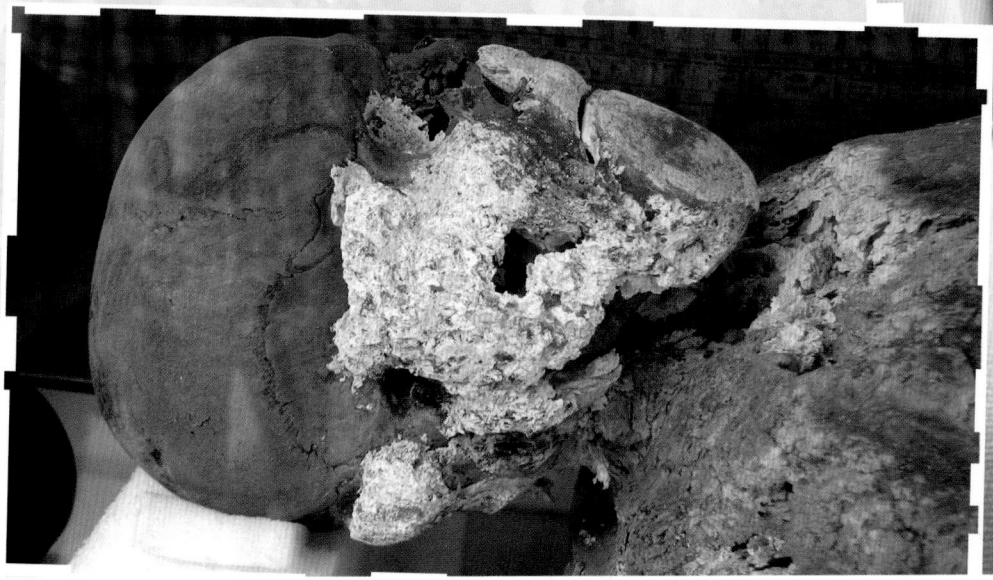

The "Soap Man" is a body preserved by adipocere.

adipocere name given to body fats when they turn soapy or waxy after death

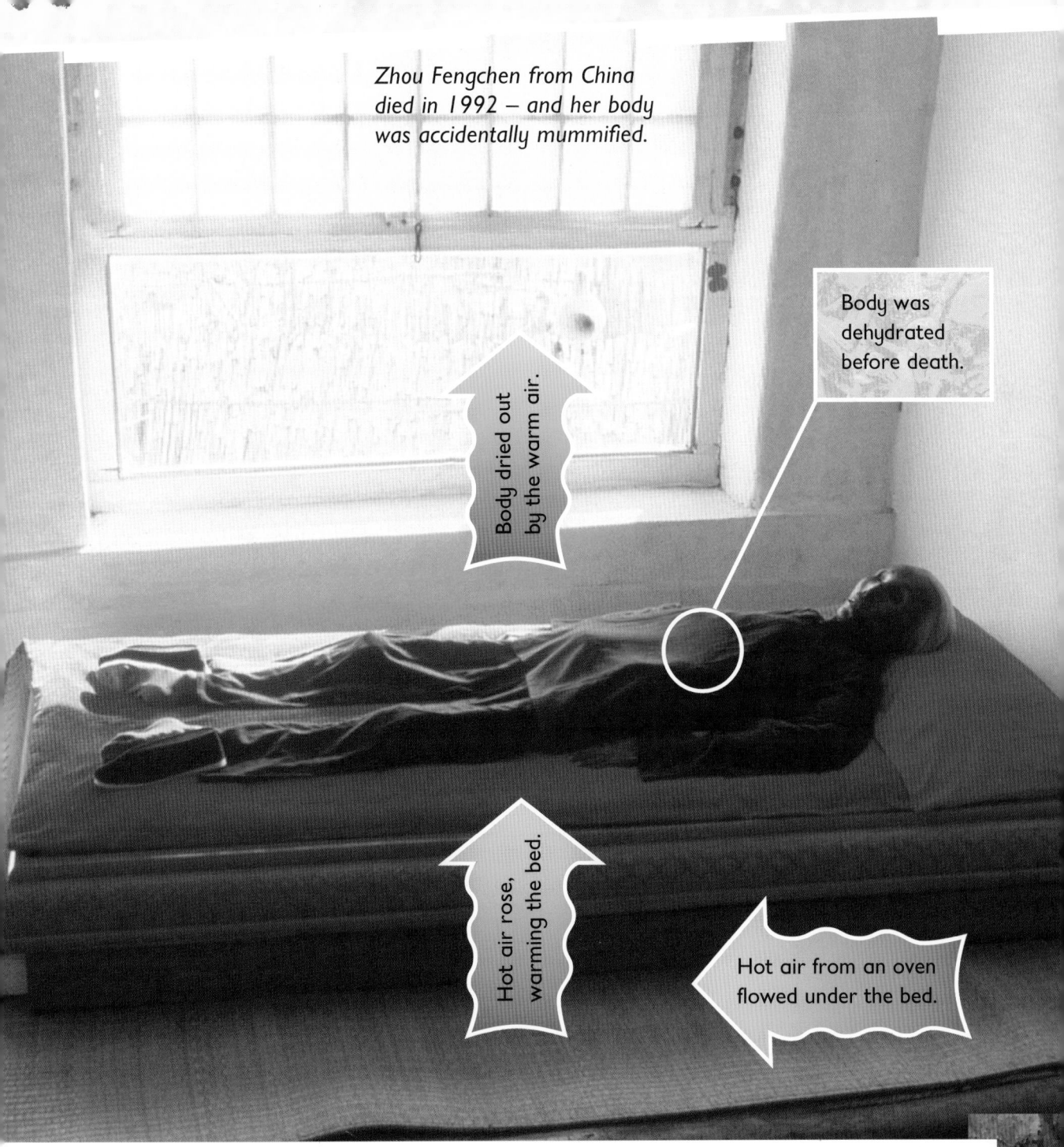

airtight sealed so that air cannot get in or out

Mummy misery

How would you like to be stuck in a glass case – in the nude – for people to stare at? That's what some mummies have to put up with!

No fuel like an old fuel

As mummies are very dry, it is claimed that some were burnt as fuel for steam trains!

Throughout history, mummies have been treated terribly by people who didn't realize (or didn't care) what they were handling:

- Mummies have been sold by **tomb** robbers to wealthy collectors.
- Some have been ground up and used in medicine.
- In Guanajuato, Mexico, people had to pay to stay buried! If relatives could not afford the fees then the bodies were dug up and put on display in a museum.

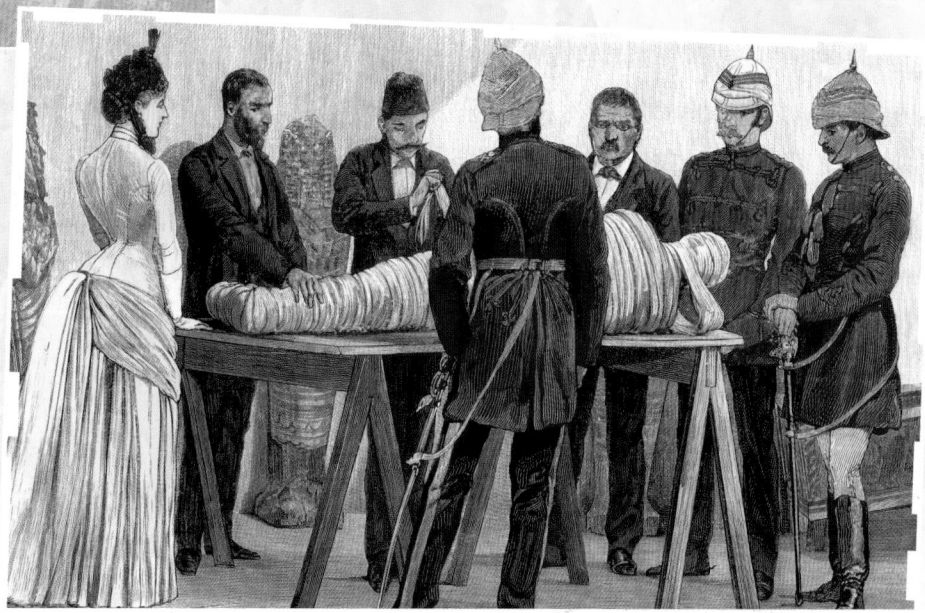

Parties to watch a mummy being unwrapped were popular in Victorian Britain.

tomb a burial chamber

This Mexican mummy from Guanajuato appears to be screaming. Could she have been buried alive?

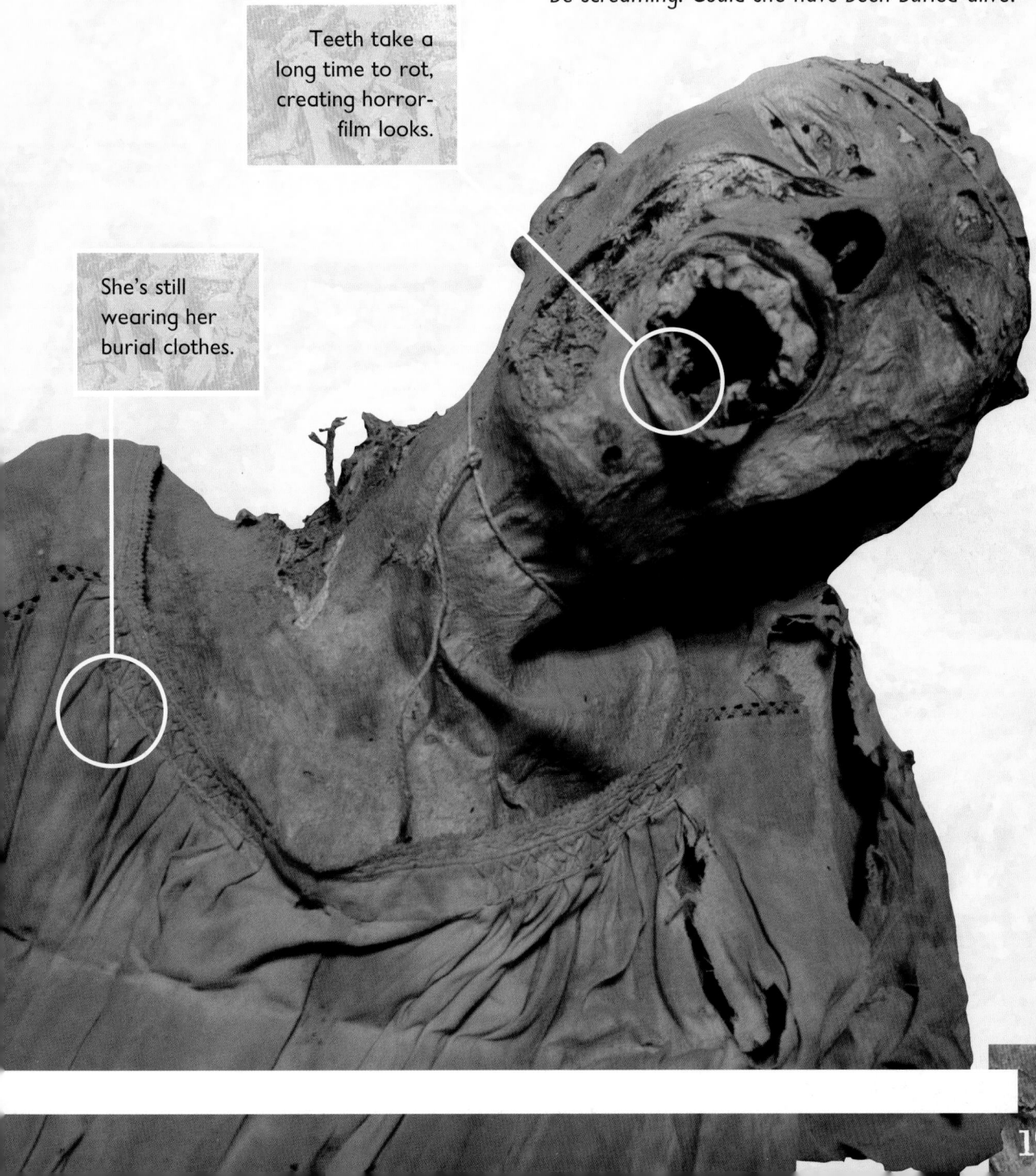

Under wraps

Taking a mummy to hospital seems a bit odd – after all, it's a bit late for a doctor to do anything. It's not too late for archaeologists, though.

Archaeologists use hi-tech hospital machinery to look inside mummies – without having to remove any bandages. **X-ray machines** and **CT scanners** beam rays of energy, called X-rays, through the mummy. Hard bits, such as bones, absorb the rays, while soft bits, such as skin, let the rays through. The results are then shown on a photograph.

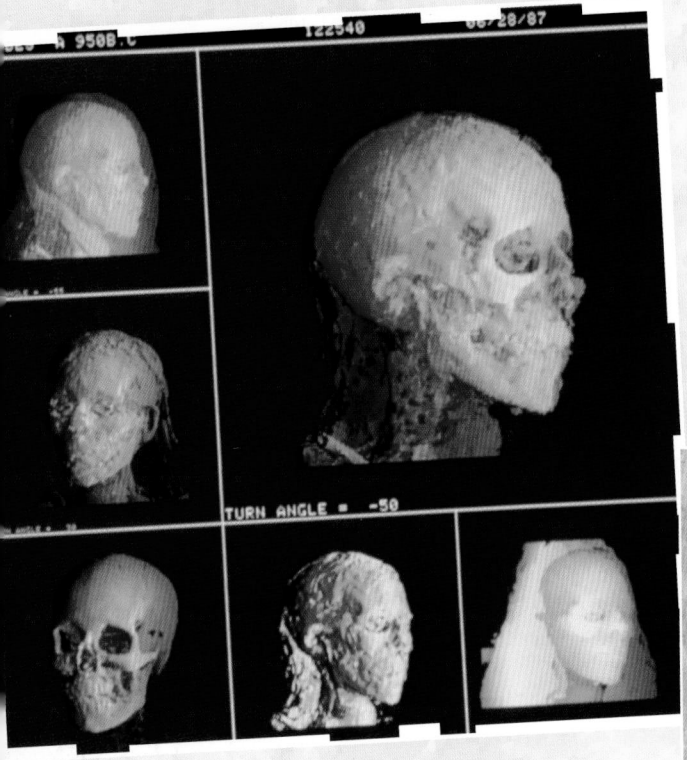

CT scans show the skull of an Egyptian mummy called Ta-bes.

Mystery solved

Many people thought that the ancient Egyptian King Tutankhamun was murdered. In fact, modern investigations found he had died from an infected leg wound.

archaeologist someone who studies ancient peoples by looking at their remains

Mummies don't even have to leave their coffins to be scanned.

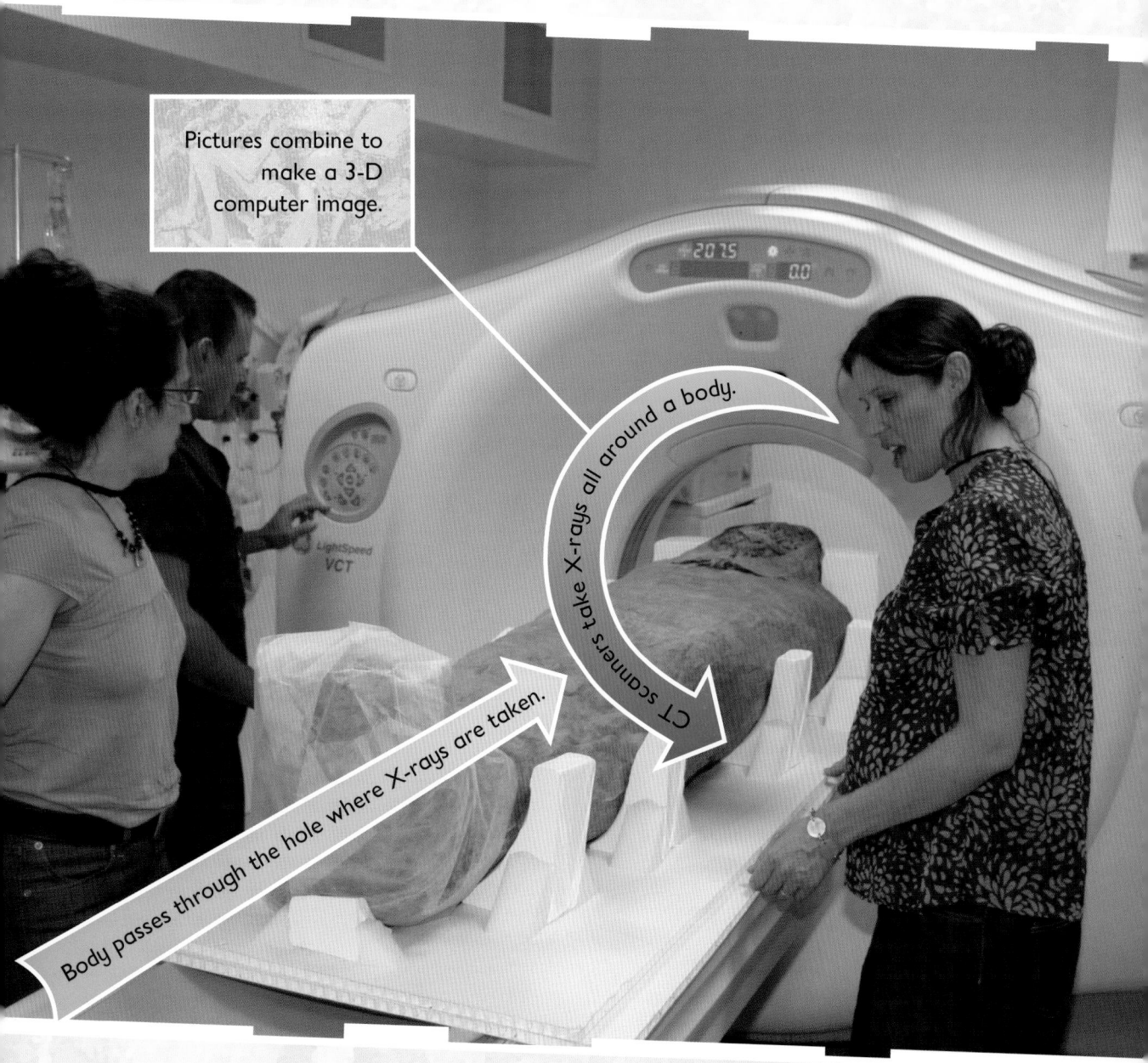

X-ray machines and **CT scanners** machines that take pictures of the inside of a body

Back from the dead

Do looks matter? Archaeologists think so, which is why they spend so much time studying mummies to work out what they might have looked like.

Reconstructions *have been made from this 2,000 year-old bog body, known as Lindow Man.*

reconstruction a copy of something that no longer survives

2 Flesh and muscles are added next, using local people as a guide to facial features.

Reconstructing the faces of people who have died is a skill that the police often use when solving crimes. It's useful for archaeologists too. They can get a good idea of what a mummy might have looked like when it was alive. Sometimes looks can tell them other things about a person, too.

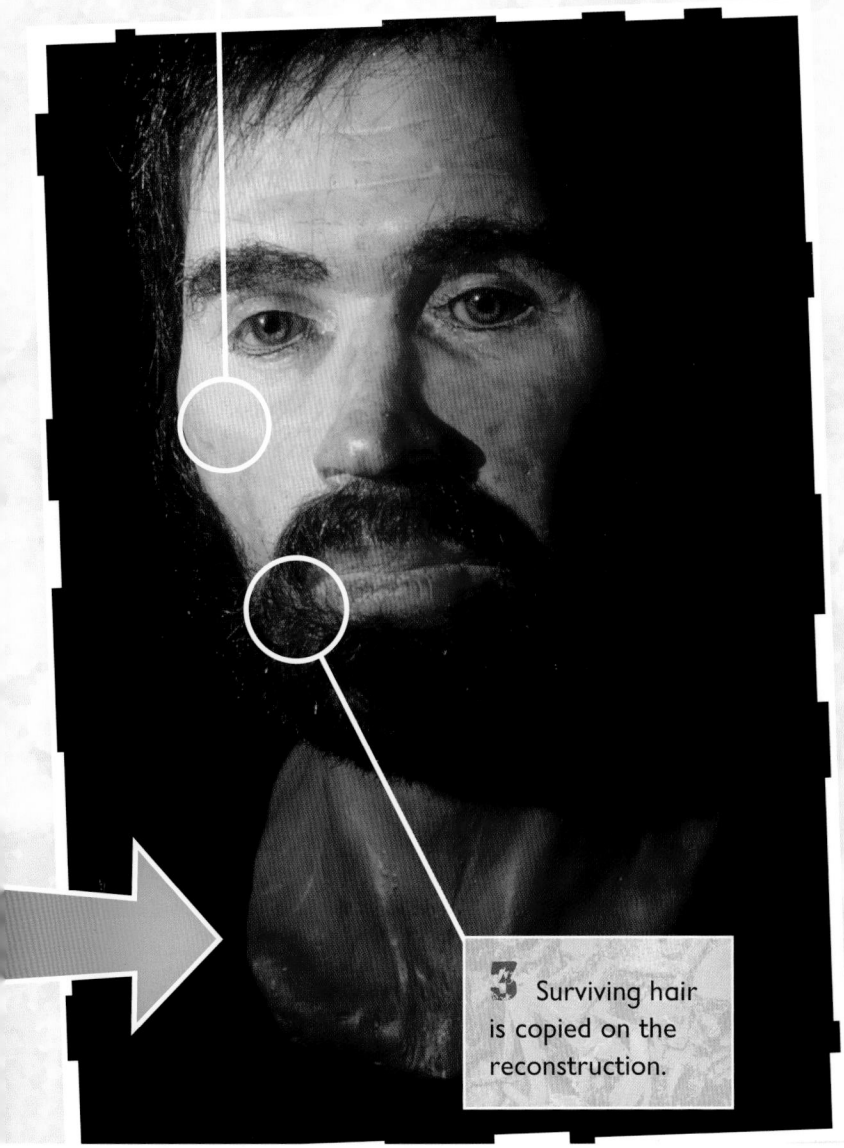

3 Surviving hair is copied on the reconstruction.

Hand history

Archaeologists look at different parts of mummies for clues about their lives. Rough hands or fingernails show that the person probably did manual work.

This is what Lindow Man might have looked like in life.

manual work working with your hands, for example farming

Celebrity mummies

Important people – including kings, priests, and even politicians – have been mummified throughout history.

Russian leader Vladimir Lenin's body is on display in Moscow.

Face and hands occasionally show signs of rotting.

My feet smell!

Jeremy Bentham's real head used to sit between the feet of his mummy.

No one really knows why the **philosopher** Jeremy Bentham wanted to be mummified. But we do know that his head fell off in the process, and had to be replaced with a wax one!

The Russian political leader Lenin had no idea that he would be mummified. On his death, the government decided to preserve his body so the Russian people could pay their respects.

State secret

We're not sure how Lenin's body was mummified – but he needs top-up treatments every year, to stop him going rotten.

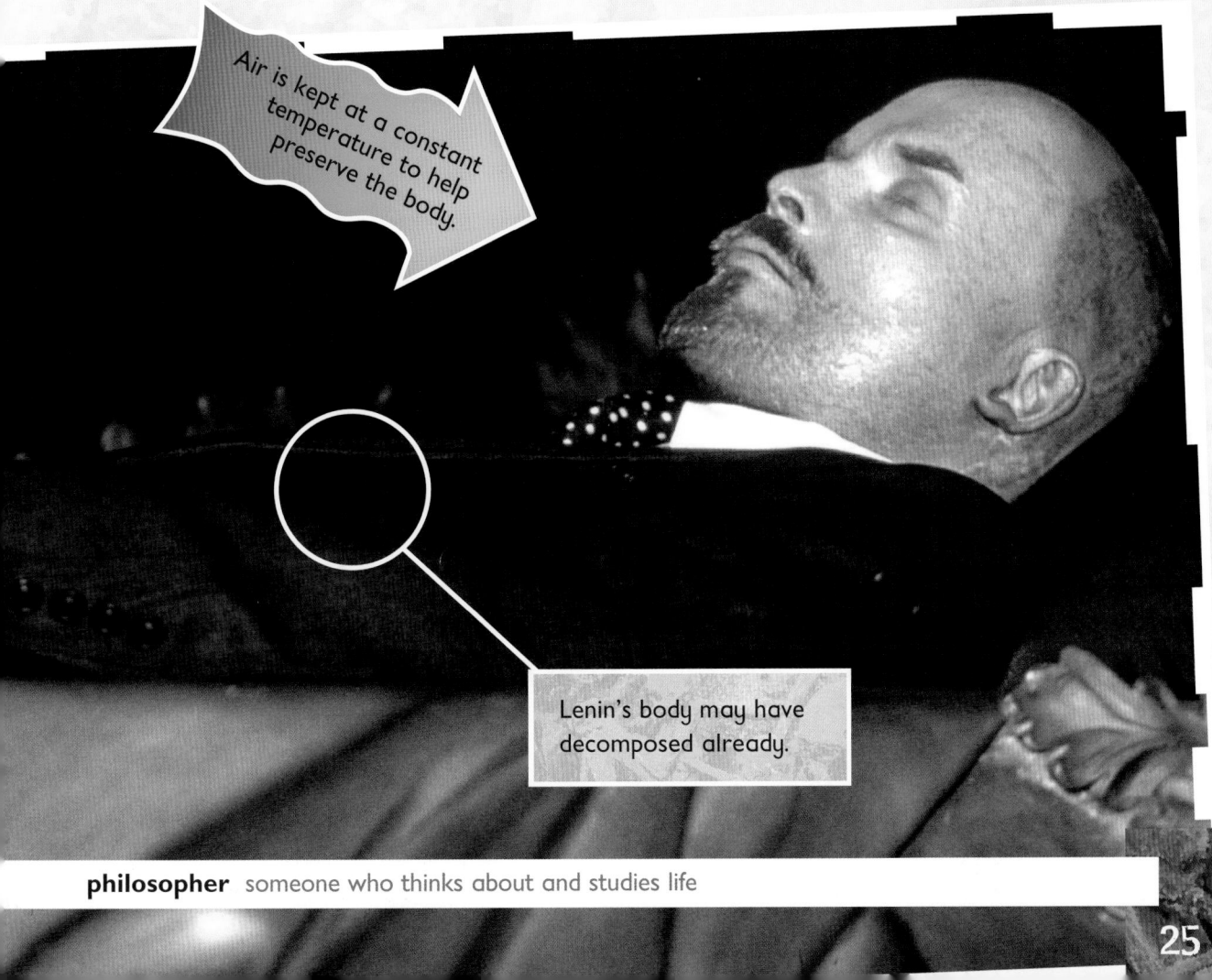

philosopher someone who thinks about and studies life

Fakes and mistakes

When is a mummy not a mummy? When it's a fake or a mistake! Sometimes mummies are not what they appear...

Occasionally museums have discovered that the mummies they have on display are actually fakes – nothing more than bandages stuffed with cloths. They had been conned!

Not all empty body coverings are fakes, though. In some cases, real attempts to mummify bodies have failed – leaving nothing but the clothes or coffin the body was buried in.

Faking a small animal mummy is easier than faking a human mummy.

jade a valuable gemstone

*A Chinese emperor once lay inside this head-to-toe **jade** suit.*

Animal antics

The Egyptians mummified animals they thought were sacred, such as cats, crocodiles and even bulls.

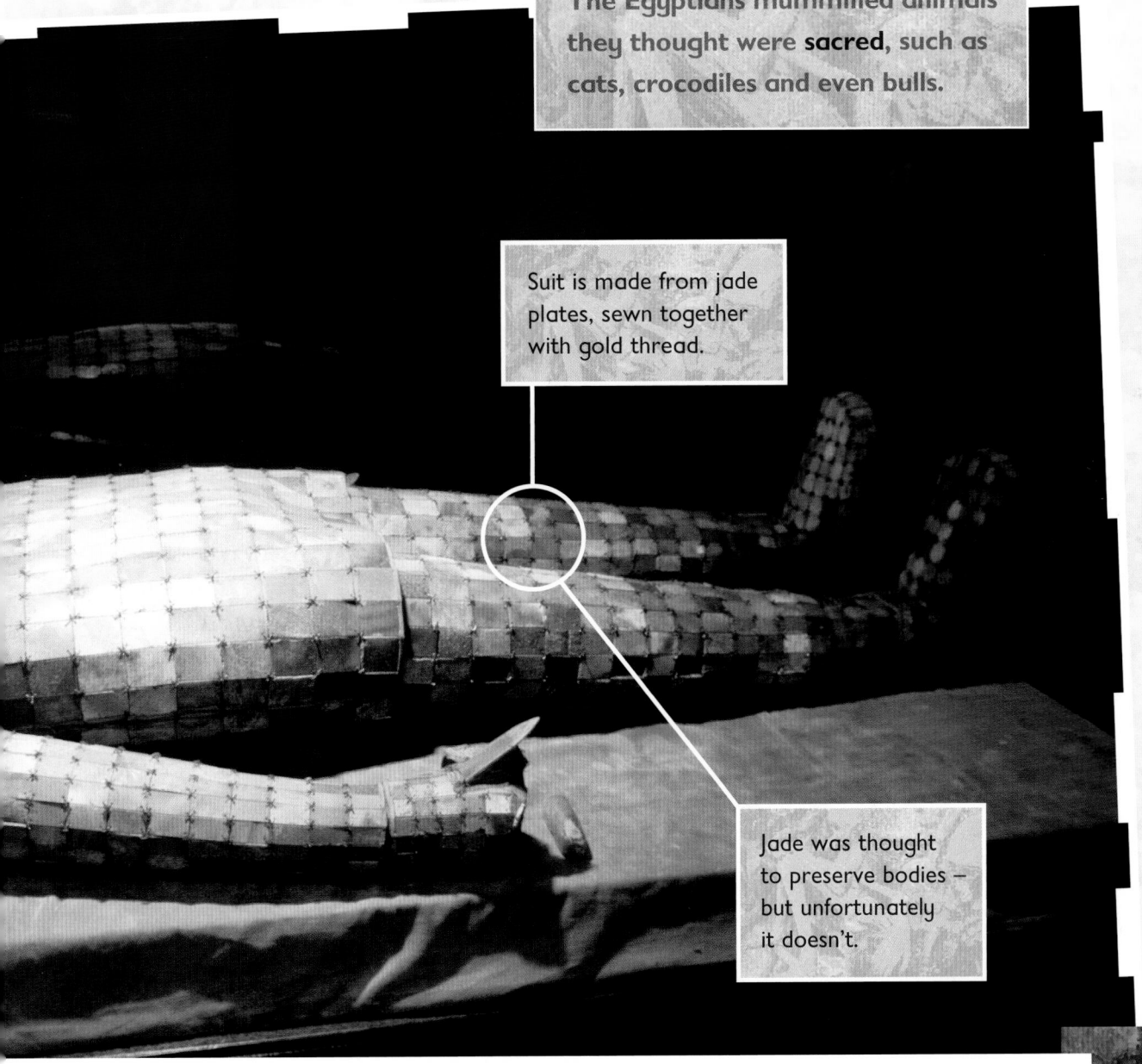

sacred important or holy in a particular religion

Modern mummies

Believe it or not, people are still being mummified today – though things have moved on since ancient Egyptian times!

A plastinated body gets ready for an exhibition.

A German professor called Gunther von Hagens has discovered a new way of making mummies. He uses a process called plastination.

Plastination works by **dissolving** all of a body's fat, and replacing the body's water with liquid plastic. Once plastinated, the mummies go on display in museums and galleries around the world. Being dead has become a great way of attracting visitors!

Plastic pets

Any living thing can be plastinated, from tiny insects to large animals such as horses.

dissolve to break down a solid in a liquid

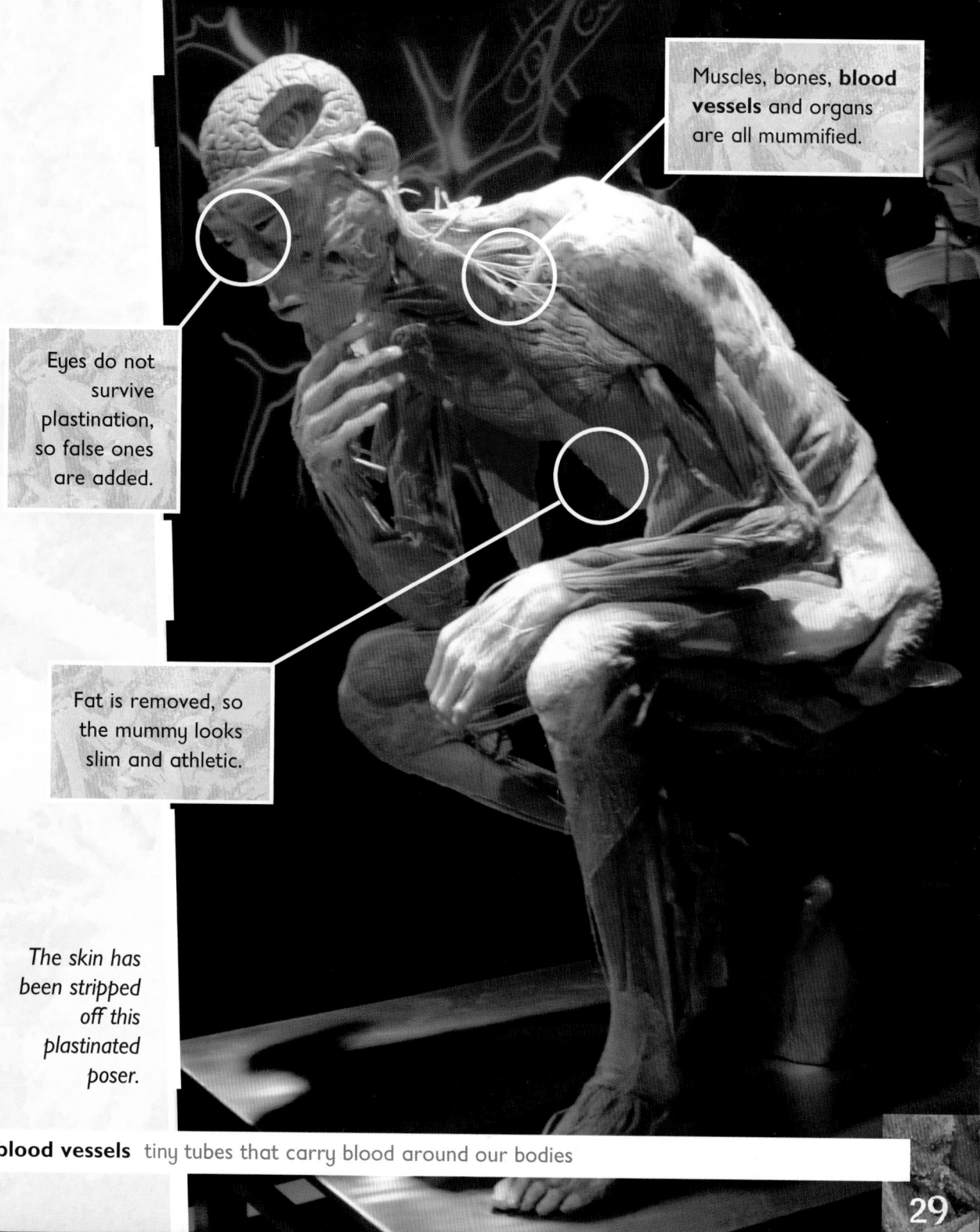

The skin has been stripped off this plastinated poser.

blood vessels tiny tubes that carry blood around our bodies

Glossary

absorb to soak up

acid substance that can cause chemical changes

adipocere name given to body fats when they turn soapy or waxy after death

afterlife life after death

airtight sealed so that air cannot get in or out

archaeologist someone who studies ancient peoples by looking at their remains

bacteria tiny cells that can both help and harm living things

blood vessels tiny tubes that carry blood around our bodies

community a group of people who live near each other

corpse a dead body

CT scanners machines that take 3-D pictures of the inside of a body

dehydrate to dry out

dissolve to break down a solid in a liquid

flint a type of stone used for old tools and weapons

intestines the tube from your stomach to your bottom

jade a valuable gemstone

manual work working with your hands, for example farming

moisture wetness

organs parts of the body that do special jobs

peat mixture of rotting plants and water

philosopher someone who thinks about and studies life

pollen a powdery substance that plants use to reproduce

preserve to keep, or make last

reconstruction a copy of something that no longer survives

sacred important or holy in a particular religion

sacrificed killed as part of a religious ceremony

tomb a burial chamber

withered dried out

X-ray machines machines that take pictures of the inside of a body

Further information

Books

Mummy by James Putnam (Dorling Kindersley, 2004)
A good overview of different types of mummy.

The Complete Book of Mummies by Claire Llewellyn (Wayland, 2001)
Looks at how mummies – including animal mummies – are made and studied.

Mummies and Pyramids by Sam Taplin (Usbourne, 2001)
Lots on Egyptian mummies as well as others – with handy internet links.

Bog Bodies: Mummies and Curious Corpses by Natalie Jane Prior (Allen and Unwin, 1996)
Discover lots of different mummies made in lots of different ways.

My Best Book of Mummies by Philip Steele (Kingfisher Books, 2000)
Good information on Egyptian mummies covering all the major areas.

Websites

www.mummytombs.com
This site describes different kinds of mummies from all over the world.

www.britishmuseum.org
Try the British Museum site for Egyptian mummies (humans and animals) and the Lindow Man.

www.carnegiemnh.org/exhibits/egypt/index.htm
The Carnegie Museum has a lot on ancient Egypt.

www.voxel-man.de/gallery/virtual_mummy/
See how a mummy can be reconstructed using a CT scanner. There is actual footage of an Egyptian mummy being scanned, along with the results.

http://video.nationalgeographic.com/video/player/specials/in-the-field-specials/ceruti-mummy.html
Watch a video about the discovery of Peruvian mummies.

Films

BEWARE! Some of these films are scary!

The Curse of the Mummy's Tomb directed by Michael Carreras (Hammer, 1964)
An old-fashioned horror film in which a mummy taken to England comes back to life.

The Mummy directed by Stephen Sommers (Universal, 1999)
Treasure hunters accidentally awaken a 3,600-year-old Egyptian mummy, with fatal results.

The Mummy: Tomb of the Dragon Emperor directed by Rob Cohen (Universal, 2008)
An action adventure. Not really about a mummy as such – more like the re-awakening of a cursed Chinese Emperor.

Index

adipocere 16
afterlife 9
animal mummies 26, 27, 28
archaeologists 20, 22, 23

bacteria 4, 11, 12
bandages 5, 9, 20, 26
Bentham, Jeremy 24, 25
bog bodies 12–13, 22
bones 4, 7, 20, 29

China 6, 17, 27
cryonics 11
CT scanners 20, 21

dried mummies 6, 7, 15, 17

Egyptians 5, 7, 8–9, 20, 27, 28

fat 16, 28, 29

hair 7, 12, 23

ice mummy 10–11

jade 26, 27

Lenin, Vladimir 24, 25
Lindow Man 22, 23

Mexico 18, 19
mummification 8–9
museums 18, 26, 28

natron 8

organs 8, 9, 29
Otzi 10–11

Papua New Guinea 14
Peru 10
Philippines 15
plastination 28–29

reconstructions 22, 23
rotting 4, 24, 25

sacrifice 12
skin 7, 13, 15, 20, 29
smoke 14, 15
Soap Man 16

teeth 4, 19
Tollund Man 13
tomb robbers 18
Tutankhamun 20

vampire legends 16
von Hagens, Gunther 28

water 6, 7, 8, 12, 28

X-ray machines 20, 21